MILITARY HEROES

ROOSEVELT'S
ROUGH
FEARLESS CAVALRY OF THE SPANISH-AMERICAN WAR
RIDERS

BY BRYNN BAKER

WITHDRAWN

CAPSTONE PRESS
a capstone imprint

Fact Finders Books are published by Capstone Press,
1710 Roe Crest Drive, North Mankato, Minnesota 56003
www.capstonepub.com

Library of Congress Cataloging-in-Publication Data
Baker, Brynn.
  Roosevelt's Rough Riders : fearless cavalry of the Spanish-American War / by Brynn Baker.
      pages cm.—(Fact finders. Military heroes.)
  Includes bibliographical references and index.
  Summary: "Discusses the heroic actions and experiences of Roosevelt's Rough Riders and the impact they made during times of war or conflict"—Provided by publisher.
  ISBN 978-1-4914-4840-3 (library binding)
  ISBN 978-1-4914-4908-0 (paperback)
  ISBN 978-1-4914-4926-4 (eBook PDF)
1. United States. Army. Volunteer Cavalry, 1st—History—Juvenile literature. 2. Roosevelt, Theodore, 1858-1919—Juvenile literature. 3. Spanish-American War, 1898—Regimental histories—Juvenile literature. 4. Spanish-American War, 1898—Cuba—Juvenile literature. [1. United States. Army. Volunteer Cavalry, 1st.] I. Title.
  E725.451st .B35 2015
  973.8'9—dc23   2015017099

Editorial Credits
Editor: Jennifer Loomis
Designer: Veronica Scott
Media Researcher: Eric Gohl
Production Specialist: Tori Abraham

Photo Credits
Alamy: 914 collection, 12 (bottom), Hi-Story, 12 (top), Historic Florida, 13; Capstone: 4; Corbis: Bettmann, 10–11; Courtesy of the National Guard Bureau: The Rough Riders, a National Guard Heritage Painting by Mort Kunstler, 24; CriaImages.com: Jay Robert Nash Collection, 5; Getty Images: Ed Vebell, 21, Nina Leen, 9, Stringer/MPI, cover; Granger, NYC: 17, 22; Library of Congress: 15, 18–19, 20, 23, 25, 27; Newscom: Everett Collection, 6, 7; Shutterstock: Everett Historical, 8
Design Elements: Shutterstock

Primary source bibliography
Page 10—Brands, H. W. *T.R.: The Last Romantic*. New York: Basic Books, 1997.
Pages 11, 13, 14, 16, 18, 21, 22, and 24—Roosevelt, Theodore. *The Rough Riders*. New York: Charles Scribner's Sons, 1899.
Page 14—Walker, Dale L. *The Boys of '98: Theodore Roosevelt and the Rough Riders*. New York: Tom Doherty Associates, Inc., 1998.
Page 26—Morris, Edmund. *The Rise of Theodore Roosevelt*. New York: Coward, McCann & Geoghegan, 1979.
Page 26—Miller, Nathan. *Theodore Roosevelt: A Life*. New York: William Morrow, 1992.

Printed in Canada.
032015   008825FRF15

TABLE OF CONTENTS

Chapter 1
SPANISH-AMERICAN WAR.. 4

Chapter 2
ROUGH RIDERS.. 10

Chapter 3
BATTLES IN CUBA... 16

Chapter 4
AMERICAN HEROES... 24

TIMELINE 28

CRITICAL THINKING USING THE COMMON CORE 29

GLOSSARY 30

READ MORE 31

INTERNET SITES 31

INDEX 32

SPANISH-AMERICAN WAR

During the late 1800s, the Spanish Empire controlled many islands around the world. Cuba, which is located off the coast of Florida, was the largest of these islands. Many Cubans wanted their freedom and independence from Spain. Cuban **guerrilla** rebels had already been fighting the Spanish for more than 20 years. The United States planned to help Cuba free itself from Spanish rule.

Cuba is located very close to the United States. The shortest distance between the two countries is about 90 miles (145 kilometers). During the late 1800s, there were many U.S. citizens living in Cuba.

The United States had more than $50 million invested in Cuba's annual sugar trade. However, the U.S. Congress had recently enacted a new sugar tariff. A tariff is a tax placed on certain foreign items that enter a country. This limited the amount of sugar that could be imported into the United States. America's investment was suffering. The change motivated the United States to fight Spain for Cuba's freedom. The United States wanted to buy Cuba once it was free. The sugar produced there would belong to the United States, so it wouldn't be subject to the tariff.

In January 1898 Cubans **rebelled** against Spanish rule. The USS *Maine*, a U.S. Navy ship, was sent to Cuba's Havana Harbor to protect American interests during the **revolution**. On February 15 a huge explosion destroyed the ship and killed 260 of the 400 men on board.

William Randolph Hearst, owner of the *New York Journal*, offered a $50,000 reward to anyone who could solve the mystery of the USS *Maine* explosion. Hearst's paper included more than eight pages a day about the explosion for weeks after the event occurred.

In March 1898 investigators for the U.S. Navy ruled that an underwater mine blew up the ship. They never directly blamed Spain, but most Americans did. Tension between the United States and Spain grew quickly.

Congress passed a law on March 9, 1898, granting $50 million to strengthen and expand the U.S. military. On April 25 President William McKinley declared war on Spain. Seventeen thousand American troops were sent to Cuba to fight in the Spanish-American War.

Was It an Accident?

In 1976 a team of American naval investigators concluded that the USS *Maine* explosion was likely caused by an accidental fire on board the ship.

THEODORE ROOSEVELT

Sitting tall on his horse, Theodore Roosevelt was hard to miss. His father had told him to "build" his body ever since he was a young boy. Roosevelt obeyed and continually pushed himself to be stronger. He lifted weights, taught himself to box, and did gymnastics.

Roosevelt grew up in New York City and later attended Harvard University from 1876 to 1880. However, after the death of his wife Alice in 1884, Roosevelt moved west to the Dakota Badlands where he bought two ranches and 1,000 cattle. Badlands are areas with little to no plant life and small, steep hills.

Roosevelt led an active lifestyle and liked to take part in outdoor adventures. He rode his horse for days on end—herding cattle, hunting grizzly bears, and chasing criminals as a frontier sheriff. His closest friends were ranch hands and cowboys. These ideal days ended when most of Roosevelt's cattle died during a long and harsh winter in 1886.

This misfortune prompted Roosevelt to return to New York where he eventually served as United States Civil Service **Commissioner**. As commissioner he created a fair hiring system for government workers. He later became the New York City Police Commissioner. Then in 1897 President McKinley appointed Roosevelt Assistant Secretary of the Navy.

One year later the United States needed more men to fight in the war against Spain. It needed at least 75,000 troops to stand a chance against the Spanish in Cuba. At the time the U.S. Army had only 28,000 soldiers. Congress approved the formation of volunteer **regiments** to help the regular army in battle. At age 40 Roosevelt gave up his job with the navy and volunteered to fight.

Secretary of War Russell Alger offered Roosevelt command of the 1st United States Volunteer Cavalry Regiment. However, Roosevelt had never held such a position and doubted his ability to lead a regiment. Roosevelt suggested his friend, Leonard Wood, for the job instead. Wood was a medical officer and President McKinley's physician.

Theodore Roosevelt (left) and Leonard Wood (right) met in 1897 while Roosevelt was working in Washington, D.C. They became close friends and worked well together. Roosevelt said he learned a lot from Wood's military experience.

Roosevelt became second in command of the volunteer regiment. People always recognized him for his proud posture while sitting on his horse. He had a bushy mustache and little, round glasses. Roosevelt wore a slouched hat, a knotted handkerchief around his neck, and leather gloves up to his elbows. His commands were loud and clear. He had a unique voice that his troops recognized and obeyed.

TEDDY'S BEAR

After not locating any bears during a 1902 bear-hunting trip in Mississippi, Theodore Roosevelt's assistants found one for him. They tied it to a tree and encouraged Roosevelt to shoot it. Roosevelt refused because of the unfairness of the situation. When a Brooklyn man who made stuffed animals read about this event, he got an idea. He created a stuffed bear in honor of Roosevelt and called it Teddy's Bear—the world's first teddy bear. More than 100 years later, teddy bears continue to be popular toys.

commissioner—an official who heads up the administration of a government department
regiment—a large group of soldiers who fights together as a unit

CHAPTER 2

ROUGH RIDERS

Men from all walks of life poured in to volunteer for the 1st United States Volunteer Cavalry Regiment. Some of the men signed up out of patriotism while others simply wanted to add some adventure to their lives. Applicants were tested for their physical strength. They needed to know how to ride a horse and shoot a gun. More than 1,000 men made up the volunteer regiment.

The recruits included polo players, football players, tennis champions, priests, doctors, lawyers, sheriffs, bakers, miners, cowboys, and American Indians. Reporters called this unusual group of soldiers the Rough Riders. "It is as typical an American regiment as ever marched or fought," Roosevelt said proudly.

In May 1898 the Rough Riders trained together at Camp Wood near San Antonio, Texas. They were given rifles, handguns, and horses. The men began each day with drills, first on foot then on horseback. The soldiers were trained to use their horses as weapons. "If my men could be trained to hit their **adversaries** with their horses, it was a matter of small amount whether or not ... revolvers were used," Roosevelt recalled in his account of the war. However, the horses were as wild as many of the soldiers. Each man had to teach his horse to obey commands.

Roosevelt (seated at the head of the table on the right) refused to accept any special treatment as second in command. He ate the same foods that were provided to the Rough Riders. Some officers slept inside camp buildings. Roosevelt chose to sleep outside in a tent, just like his men. It was important to Roosevelt to live in the same manner that his soldiers lived.

adversary—someone who fights or argues against you

MEET SOME ROUGH RIDERS

Dr. James Robb Church was a Princeton football player who served as the Rough Riders' surgeon.

John Campbell Greenway was a Yale football player and baseball player.

David Marvin Goodrich was captain of Harvard's rowing team.

Captain Bucky O'Neill was a tough sheriff and gambler from Arizona before being killed during battle in the Spanish-American War.

William "Little Billy" McGinty was an expert horse trainer from the West.

Captain Bucky O'Neill

At first Theodore Roosevelt and Leonard Wood didn't like the name Rough Riders. It wasn't until the name was used in formal military communications that the two men accepted it. The regiment was also briefly known as Teddy's Terrors and Wood's Weary Walkers.

READY FOR ACTION

The Rough Riders quickly completed training and were prepared for battle. On May 29, 1898, the volunteer soldiers left camp and boarded a train to Tampa, Florida. They wore blue flannel shirts and light-brown pants, boots, and hats. Many also wore loosely knotted, red handkerchiefs around their necks. The uniforms suited the rugged American men well.

People cheered for the regiment at train stations along the way. "Everywhere we saw the stars and stripes," Roosevelt recalled. Many gave the soldiers gifts of flowers, fruits, and milk to enjoy on their journey.

The Rough Riders spent about five days in Tampa, Florida. During their time there, they trained for battle during the day. When they had free time, they rested, cleaned their weapons, told stories, and played cards and baseball.

The Rough Riders were excited to arrive in Tampa. They planned to board one of the ships headed for the battle in Cuba. However, the ship they ended up with, the *Yucatan*, did not have enough room for all the men. More than 400 Rough Riders had to stay behind. There was also not enough room on board the ship for many of their horses. Most Rough Riders would now have to fight on foot. Roosevelt wrote, "I saw more than one, both officers and privates, burst into tears when he found out he could not go."

> *"We had come a long way together and being left out at the last moment was not something any of us had counted on."*
>
> —Rough Rider Frank Brito remembering his disappointment when he was left behind in Tampa

The Rough Riders finally arrived in Cuba after several delays in Tampa and six days at sea. They were ordered to march inland, alongside America's regular army regiments and **Buffalo Soldiers**. Their task was to attack Spanish troops positioned high on Kettle and San Juan Hills near the city of Santiago.

Buffalo Soldier—an African-American soldier serving in the western United States after the Civil War

SWIMMING TO SHORE

After boarding, the ships to Cuba were delayed a week. There had been rumors of Spanish ships hiding in the sea between Florida and Cuba. The American ships sat in the harbor until the route was declared safe. When the ships arrived in Cuba, there were not enough rowboats to carry the men and gear to Cuban shores. Many of the men were expected to swim the last half-mile (0.8 kilometer) or so to shore. The sea was rough and at least two men drowned.

The Rough Riders waited on the *Yucatan* in Port Tampa for almost a week. The conditions on board were cramped, hot, and dirty. There was no space to train for battle so there was little to do. The men were given canned beef for food. It tasted terrible, and even though they were hungry, most of the men refused to eat it. Despite these challenging conditions, Roosevelt said his men remained positive and didn't complain.

CHAPTER 3

BATTLES IN CUBA

The Rough Riders participated in their first battle of the Spanish-American War just two days after arriving in Cuba. On June 24, 1898, the Rough Riders walked up a muddy trail in Las Guásimas, Cuba, and were met with heavy gunfire. On their left was flooded, grassy land and on their right, a jungle thick with trees. Spanish soldiers hid in the landscape, firing bullets and cannons at the exposed Americans.

For several minutes the Rough Riders could not see the Spanish troops. "There they are," said Richard Harding Davis, a journalist who was writing about the Spanish-American War. "Look over there, I can see their hats." Quietly pointing across the valley to the right, Roosevelt had his best men fire back. The Spanish soldiers sprang from their cover while the Rough Riders and other U.S. soldiers pushed forward. Outnumbered, the Spanish troops soon **retreated**.

However short, the Battle of Las Guásimas was still costly. Sixteen American soldiers were killed, eight of them Rough Riders. The regiments buried their dead the next day in a mass grave. Roosevelt said, "There could be no more honorable burial than these men in a common grave—Indian and cowboy, miner, packer, and college athlete." After the battle Roosevelt was made colonel and given full command of the Rough Riders.

Roosevelt pressured the army to give the Rough Riders the same weapons that regular army regiments used. Even though they were a volunteer unit, Roosevelt thought his soldiers were just as good as regular soldiers.

retreat—to move back or withdraw from a difficult situation

That night the Rough Riders camped in a grassy marsh near a stream. They waited there for further orders, but days passed with no word. Cavalry trumpets woke the men each morning, and every night the different regiments played the "Star-Spangled Banner." "Officers and men alike stood with heads uncovered, wherever they were, until the last strains of the anthem died away in the hot sunset air," Roosevelt recalled in his autobiography.

Spanish Weapons

Spanish troops used smokeless gunpowder, making it difficult for the Americans to locate them.

The Buffalo Soldiers played an important role in the Battle of Las Guásimas. When the Rough Riders became trapped by Spanish gunfire, the Buffalo Soldiers' 10th Cavalry Regiment rushed to the scene and fired back. They helped force the Spanish soldiers away from Las Guásimas. Although the Buffalo Soldiers weren't given as much recognition as the Rough Riders, their participation in the Spanish-American War was just as important.

THE BATTLE AT KETTLE HILL

On the morning of June 30, 1898, Roosevelt received orders to advance his troops to Santiago. He ordered his men to pack a **canteen** full of water and three days' worth of food. The Rough Riders marched all day, many without their horses. The jungle heat was intense and exhausting. As they neared Santiago on July 1, they came upon a sunken trail that led them between Kettle and San Juan Hills.

Spanish soldiers fired down on them from the top of Kettle Hill. The Spanish troops **camouflaged** themselves in the jungle and perched high up in the trees. Roosevelt's Rough Riders were caught in heavy gunfire and did not see the attack coming. Captain Bucky O'Neill was shot in the head and killed. The Rough Riders ran through the gunfire while crouching low and proceeded to Kettle Hill on their right. Roosevelt took the lead on his horse, Texas.

When the Rough Riders arrived in Cuba, there was no good way to get their horses onto land. The animals were thrown overboard from the ship they were traveling on into the water below. Both of Leonard Wood's horses made it to shore. One of Theodore Roosevelt's horses drowned.

Another challenge the Rough Riders faced was the discomfort of their uniforms. Their dark-blue shirts were made out of wool, which was too hot for the Cuban climate.

The men approached a regular U.S. Army captain and his troops. Roosevelt asked the captain if he was waiting for orders to advance up Kettle Hill. When the captain said yes, Roosevelt responded, "Then I am the ranking officer here and I give the order to charge."

The captain hesitated to obey because the order did not come from his colonel. "Then let my men through, sir," Roosevelt ordered. He rode tall on his horse while crossing Spanish lines, followed by his loyal Rough Riders. "It proved too much for the regulars," Roosevelt recalled. "So they jumped up and came along." The American troops fearlessly charged Kettle Hill. The men cheered and pushed forward between gunshots. The Rough Riders won the battle and took control of the first hill. However, they were still under fire from off in the distance.

canteen—a small, portable metal container for holding water or other liquids
camouflage—coloring or covering that makes animals, people, and objects look like their surroundings

Famous Charge up
San Juan Hill

The Spanish still controlled San Juan Hill, the higher of the two peaks. "I called for the men to charge the next line of trenches on the hills to our front," Roosevelt noted. "Follow me, boys!" he ordered.

Roosevelt and his men leaped over a wire fence and sprinted across the wide valley separating the two hills. Roosevelt led his men on the second uphill charge that made them famous.

The Spanish-American War was one of the shortest in American history. It lasted 113 days. In a July 1898 letter to Roosevelt, the war was described as "a splendid little war" by Ambassador to Great Britain John Hay.

It was not long before the Spanish saw the relentless blue wave of soldiers rushing toward them. Outnumbered once again, the Spanish troops retreated to Santiago. American soldiers swarmed the top of San Juan Hill and took control.

The battle only lasted a day, yet it became one of the most famous in American history. Within weeks the Spanish at Santiago surrendered to the U.S. Army. The Rough Riders' successful advance up San Juan Hill became the key victory in winning the Spanish-American War.

America had an estimated total of 274,000 soldiers in Cuba during the Spanish-American War. About 560 of those soldiers were Rough Riders. Twenty-five Rough Riders died during battle and 19 died from disease. Their regiment lost more men than any other army unit of similar size. The total number of American soldiers killed during combat was less than 400.

On July 3, 1898, two days after their defeat at San Juan Hill, the Spanish tried to leave Cuba. However, U.S. forces destroyed all of their ships. On July 17 Spanish troops surrendered at Santiago.

CHAPTER 4

AMERICAN HEROES

The defeat in Cuba caused the Spanish to lose control of their overseas empire. Spain and the United States signed a peace treaty on December 10, 1898, establishing Cuba's independence. Spain also surrendered the islands of Puerto Rico and Guam to the United States. Spain allowed the United States to purchase the Philippines for $20 million. The United States quickly became a world power and played a greater role in international affairs.

Roosevelt and the Rough Riders returned to the United States after months away and were hailed as heroes. Roosevelt remembered his volunteer soldiers as "a regiment of as gallant fighters as ever wore the United States uniform."

After the war some Rough Riders could not return to work right away because of sickness or injury. Wealthy supporters of the regiment offered them money. Some men accepted and used the money to help them get by until they regained their health. Other men were too proud to accept the help.

DEADLY DISEASES

Deadly diseases were the biggest cause of death during the Spanish-American War. The total number of soldiers killed during combat and from wounds totaled 345. The number of soldiers who died from disease totaled 2,565. The most common diseases included yellow fever and malaria, which were common in Cuba's warm climate. Yellow fever is an illness that can cause high fever, chills, nausea, and kidney and liver failure. Liver failure causes the skin to become yellow, giving the disease its name. Malaria is a serious disease that people get from mosquito bites. The disease causes high fever, chills, and sometimes death.

Camp Wikoff

When Roosevelt and the Rough Riders returned to the United States after the war, they stayed at Camp Wikoff on Long Island, New York. The camp was built as a place for soldiers to recover from war wounds and illness. Because the camp was located far away from the public, the soldiers couldn't spread the deadly diseases they caught in Cuba. It wasn't necessary for Roosevelt to be there. However, to show his support for the soldiers, he stayed at the camp with them.

The victory in Cuba brought Roosevelt national fame. Roosevelt soon became an unstoppable force in American politics. In 1900 he was elected vice president of the United States. When President McKinley was assassinated in 1901, Roosevelt became the 26th president. He served until 1909.

The nation and the world will always remember Roosevelt and the brave Rough Riders. "I will talk about the regiment forever," Roosevelt recalled fondly.

"Nothing can take away the fact that . . . I commanded the regiment and led it victoriously in a hard-fought battle. San Juan was the great day of my life."

—*Theodore Roosevelt proudly recalling the Rough Riders' victory at San Juan Hill*

Roosevelt visited San Antonio, Texas, for his third and final time in 1905 when he was president of the United States. He attended a Rough Riders two-day reunion with about 50 former soldiers.

TIMELINE

October 27, 1858
Theodore Roosevelt is born in New York City.

1897
Roosevelt is appointed Assistant Secretary of the U.S. Navy.

February 15, 1898
USS *Maine* explodes in Havana Harbor.

April 25, 1898
U.S. Congress declares war on Spain.

May 1898
The Rough Riders begin training at Camp Wood in Texas.

June 22, 1898
The Rough Riders arrive in Cuba.

June 24, 1898
The Rough Riders win their first battle in Las Guásimas, Cuba.

July 1, 1898
Roosevelt leads the Rough Riders to victory atop Kettle and San Juan Hills.

July 17, 1898
Spanish troops surrender at Santiago.

December 10, 1898
The Spanish-American War officially ends when the Treaty of Paris is signed.

September 14, 1901
Roosevelt becomes the 26th president of the United States.

CRITICAL THINKING USING THE COMMON CORE

1. Who were the Rough Riders? What effect did they have on the Spanish-American War? (Integration of Knowledge and Ideas)

2. Describe the events that occurred on July 1, 1898, that led to the United States winning the Spanish-American War. (Key Ideas and Details)

3. How do the events described in the timeline show how Theodore Roosevelt worked his way to becoming president of the United States? (Craft and Structure)

GLOSSARY

adversary (AD-ver-ser-ee)—someone who fights or argues against you

Buffalo Soldier (BUHF-uh-loh SOLE-jur)—an African-American soldier serving in the western United States after the Civil War

camouflage (KA-muh-flahzh)—coloring or covering that makes animals, people, and objects look like their surroundings

canteen (kan-TEEN)—a small, portable metal container for holding water or other liquids

commissioner (kuh-MI-shuh-nuhr)—an official who heads up the administration of a government department

guerrilla (guh-RIL-ah)—a soldier who is not part of a country's regular army

rebel (ri-BEL)—to fight against a government or the people in charge of something

regiment (REJ-uh-muhnt)—a large group of soldiers who fights together as a unit

retreat (ri-TREET)—to move back or withdraw from a difficult situation

revolution (rev-uh-LOO-shun)—an uprising by a group of people against a system of government or a way of life

READ MORE

Adler, David A. *Colonel Theodore Roosevelt.* New York: Holiday House, 2014.

Fitzpatrick, Brad. *Theodore Roosevelt.* New York: Chelsea House, 2011.

Hollihan, Kerrie Logan. *Theodore Roosevelt for Kids: His Life and Times, 21 Activities.* Chicago: Chicago Review Press, 2010.

Rappaport, Doreen. *To Dare Mighty Things: The Life of Theodore Roosevelt.* New York: Disney/Hyperion Books, 2013.

INTERNET SITES

FactHound offers a safe, fun way to find Internet sites related to this book. All of the sites on FactHound have been researched by our staff.

Here's all you do:
Visit **www.facthound.com**
Type in this code: 9781491448403

INDEX

Alger, Russell, 8

Buffalo Soldiers, 14, 19

Camp Wood, 11
Cuba
    Havana Harbor, 5
    Kettle Hill, 14, 20, 21
    Las Guásimas, 16, 19
    San Juan Hill, 14, 20, 22–23, 26
    Santiago, 14, 20, 23

Davis, Richard Harding, 16

1st United States Volunteer Cavalry
    Regiment, 8, 10

Guam, 24

horses, 7, 9, 10, 11, 12, 14, 20, 21

malaria, 25
McKinley, William, 6, 8, 26

peace treaties, 24
Philippines, 24
Puerto Rico, 24

reunions, 26
Rough Riders
    Brito, Frank, 14
    Church, Dr. James Robb, 12
    Goodrich, David Marvin, 12
    Greenway, John Campbell, 12
    McGinty, William "Little Billy", 12
    O'Neill, Bucky, 12, 20

Spain, 4, 5, 6, 8, 24
sugar tariffs, 5

USS *Maine*, 5, 6

Wood, Leonard, 8, 12, 20

yellow fever, 24